The Story of
Castles

Lesley Sims

Illustrated by
Teri Gower

Reading Consultant: Alison Kelly
Roehampton University

Contents

Chapter 1

The first castle

Everyone knows that fairytale kings and queens live in castles. But, only 1,000 years ago, real lords and ladies lived in them too. It all began when...

"FIRE!"

Raiders from the far north sailed down and attacked villages across Europe.

Not again!

Panic spread faster than fires
from the flaming arrows...

...until, one day, a wealthy lord had an idea.

He offered to protect the villagers in return for their land.

The lord knew his soldiers would have to move fast. So, he gathered some of them together and gave them an order.

His soldiers not only raced to any villages in trouble, they also tried to be good and kind to all.

"I'll call you knights," said the lord, "and you'll always save the day!"

Now the lord needed somewhere safe for his knights to live. He needed a castle.

"We should build by a river, so we have water..." he thought, "near trees so we have wood..."

"...and we'd better add an extra-strong fort, just in case we have to retreat."

I can see for miles!

Then the lord had a brainwave. "Let's put the fort on a hill!"

When his castle was finished, the lord was delighted. There was a hall where everyone could eat, a chapel to pray for victory and stables for the horses... all surrounded by a high fence.

A bridge led up the hill to a
wooden tower where the knights
could live. The castle became so
popular, every lord wanted one.

But the lords soon realized wooden castles had drawbacks. The plain fact was – wood was no good.

"We need stone!" they decided.

"Stop right there!" cried the king, who thought lords with stone castles and knights might become too powerful. "If you want to build in stone, you must ask me first."

So they did.

My castle is going to have a round tower.

How modern.

He's crazy.

Chapter 2

Set in stone

With the king's permission, a lord could get to work. Or, rather, he could hire a Master Mason to do the work for him.

14

The Master Mason found a site,
drew up plans and hired workmen.
Building a castle could take years...

...and one was never enough. Many
lords ended up with several.

Some lords built such vast towers, there was room for everything inside. From the outside, you could only see solid walls and narrow holes for windows. But if you could have seen through the walls...

17

Of course, there were always lords who wanted to try something different. In one place, the fashion might be for round towers.

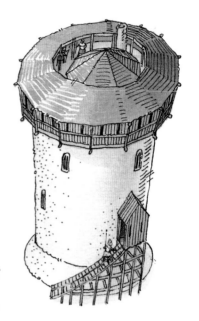

Another lord might build a tower with six, eight or even ten sides.

And a few lords didn't have a tower at all. They simply replaced their old wooden fences with stone walls. Instead of being piled on top of each other, the rooms stood in separate buildings in the grounds.

Whatever they built, lords built big. From the outside, their castles looked magnificent. Inside, they looked splendid too.

Decorators splashed gold paint over beams and hung tapestries, as large as giant posters, on the walls. They painted zigzags on pillars and stars on the ceiling.

Candles flickered in corners and
the lord's family emblem, set in a
shield, was stuck over everything.

21

"What a splendid castle!" visitors sighed. But, as they soon found out, living in one wasn't so great. In fact, it was dark, noisy, cold and often smelly.

Most windows were tiny, to keep out attackers, but they also kept out light. The only heat came from open fires, but they didn't heat the rooms that much. They billowed out smoke as well.

And, all day long, footsteps clattered up and down stone stairs. Heavy wooden doors banged shut. Servants shouted, pages whistled, babies cried and dogs barked, echoing around the stone walls.

But it's safe!

For such huge buildings, there wasn't much space inside either. Almost everything took place in one room – the Great Hall.

It was where everyone ate...

24

...where the lord and his stewards worked...

...and where some servants even slept.

Lords, at least, had a private room to share with their families. Anyone else wanting a quiet chat had to sit in a window seat.

But even the lord didn't have a bathroom. When his lady wanted a bath, servants brought water to her room and heated it over the fire. The toilets were simply holes in the wall, sometimes hidden only by a curtain.

Chapter 3

A safe house

"Never mind being private," said the lords. They had a more important question on their minds. How well would their castles defend them?

It was the first thing a lord thought about when planning his castle. He had to stop attackers from getting too close. If he could build on a high cliff, he would. If not, he had a deep moat dug around the castle walls.

As more castles went up, lords built stronger gatehouses to protect a castle's main entrance.

"That's not enough," said some. "Add a trap!" So, heavy iron gates rattled down to block off either end of the gatehouse.

But then they had to fight the trapped knights. So, holes were left in the gatehouse roof, for soldiers to throw stones and arrows through.

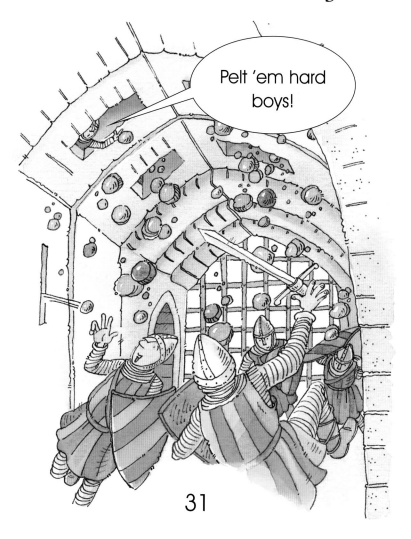

A lord would also have a drawbridge over his moat. At the first sign of trouble, guards could draw it up, sealing the castle shut.

On the top of their castles, lords had battlements. These had gaps for the knights to fire weapons through and, just as important, solid parts for them to duck behind.

Gotcha!

Lords had slits built into the walls too. Arrows could be fired out, but the holes were too thin for anything to be fired in.

Then one lord decided he wanted an extension – halfway up the outside wall. He built a long wooden cabin along one side. This had gaps in the floor for soldiers to throw down boiling hot rocks.

Everyone wanted one. Soon, most castles had a wooden extension of some kind. Only then did the lords remember – wood was no good.

So, when their wooden extensions had been smashed to smithereens or burned to cinders, they built them again... in stone.

As far as defending themselves went, lords thought they had everything covered. But a big change was coming.

Chapter 4

The new castles

Knights who had been fighting wars abroad were returning with stories of an amazing wall. This was actually three walls, one in front of the other.

Castle builders may well have heard the knights' tales, because the next castles to be built had walls within walls.

We could call it a concentric castle! No, that'll never catch on...

Now, life was twice as hard for any attackers trying to break in. Even better, from the lord's point of view, he had two rows of soldiers firing arrows at the enemy.

These latest castles were better inside as well. The extra walls had lots of towers, all with rooms, so visitors could stay.

Even without guests, space was useful because enough people lived in a castle to fill a village. There were the lord, his wife and children, the lord's servants, the lady's maids and the children's nurse.

Then there were the lord's right-hand men, his stewards. They took charge of cooks, clerks, carpenters, cleaners, ushers, gardeners and grooms.

There was a constable to take charge of the castle if the lord was away and boss the knights around.

Tidy up those shields!

Clean those swords.

Polish that chainmail.

And there were blacksmiths to make weapons, carpenters to build and fix furniture, and huntsmen to catch food.

In fact, nearly everything the lord needed could be found within the castle walls.

As time went on, lords began to want more comfort and filled their castles with grand furniture. The fancier castles even had carpets — but only hanging on the walls. And in the gardens, ladies grew flowers as well as vegetables.

But no one ever forgot a castle's main purpose was to defend against attack.

Chapter 5

Under attack!

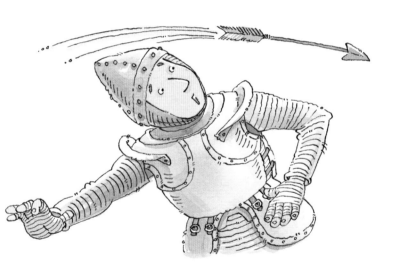

Every so often, one lord would take a liking to another lord's castle – and its land – and try to take them by force.

His attackers fired arrows and
bolts from enormous crossbows. Up
in the castle, knights would throw
every missile they could get their
hands on.

But, if the enemy surrounded the castle and refused to budge, the people inside were stuck.

The attackers were determined to get into the castle somehow. One knight even climbed up a toilet chute to let his friends in. Knights also dug tunnels under the walls to get inside.

To get into Rochester Castle, King John of England filled a tunnel with forty dead pigs. When these were set on fire, the blaze brought down the tunnel and a chunk of castle wall.

Knights inside a castle put
bowls of water on the ground floor.
Anyone seeing a ripple on the
surface of the water shouted the
alarm.

Ripples meant the
enemy was digging underfoot.
The knights started on their own
tunnel at once, ready to fight it
out underground.

A trapped lord was always worried that his food or water would run out. So, secret passages were often built into castles, which let servants sneak in with supplies.

A lord could also use the passage to send his knights on a surprise attack. Once, a spy discovered that the enemy soldiers all sat down to dinner at the same time, leaving no one on guard.

The castle knights rushed out and attacked the men as they ate.

Lords spent days thinking up tricks to fool each other. Inside a castle, knights would put dummies on the roof, to make it look as if the place was full of soldiers.

Outside, enemy knights might dress up as peasants and pretend to bring a delivery.

Once, a queen named Matilda was trapped in a castle by her cousin, King Stephen.

When winter came, Matilda had a daring idea. She dressed from top to toe in white and fled across the frozen moat, hidden by the snow.

To beat their enemies, lords and ladies didn't only need strong castles. They needed good ideas and great bravery as well.

When they won, they held huge feasts to celebrate.

Inside the kitchen, it looked as if the fight was still going on. Cooks shouted, pots boiled and servants rushed from cupboard to cauldron.

Feasts took place – where else but the Great Hall. When the lord and lady had sat down at the top table, the priest read a prayer.

Then the lord stood up and held his goblet high. "My friends," he cried, "let the feast begin!"

And what a feast it was. Pages carried in dishes piled high with stuffed peacocks, roast swans and spiced venison pie.

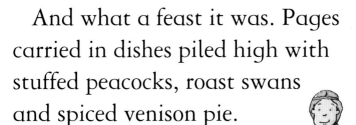

There were roasted pigs crammed with chestnuts and cheese...

cakes in wine sauce...

...and wonderful models made entirely from marzipan.

People ate until they were full, and then they ate some more. Servants ran around clearing empty plates, dodging between acrobats, jugglers and dancers.

Up above them all, musicians plucked their lutes and sang songs so jolly, the diners didn't even notice splinters in their bottoms from the rough wooden benches.

The jester told stories and everyone laughed and sang well into the night.

Chapter 6

The end

But the fun couldn't last. First, the cannon was invented. It was soon strong enough to blast holes in the biggest castle. Then lords stopped fighting each other and banded together to fight other countries.

Finally, lords and ladies decided
they didn't want to live in cold,
dark, noisy castles. They wanted
grand homes instead.

So, they stopped building castles altogether. Castles had their stones stolen for new buildings, or were simply left to collapse.

Hundreds of years went by...

...until today, when very few castles are lived in at all. Some have completely disappeared. But you don't have to look far to find a ruin, just waiting to be explored.

With thanks to Abigail Wheatley

Designed by
Russell Punter

This edition first published in 2006 by Usborne Publishing Ltd.,
Usborne House, 83-85 Saffron Hill, London EC1N 8RT, England.
www.usborne.com
Copyright © 2006, 2004 Usborne Publishing Ltd.